Don't Worry, Be Happy

Bobby McFerrin

Illustrated by Bennett Carlson

Delacorte
Press

Published by
Delacorte Press
Bantam Doubleday Dell Publishing Group, Inc.
666 Fifth Avenue
New York, New York 10103

Designed and Illustrated by Bennett Carlson

ISBN: 0 - 385 - 29802 -1

Manufactured in the United States of America
Published simultaneously in Canada

February 1989

10 9 8 7 6 5 4 3 2 1

This book is dedicated
to those dedicated to changing the world
by changing themselves.

Foreword

I believe that life is fundamentally benevolent and people are basically good and know what's good for 'em. Things just have a way of righting themselves without much meddling. No matter what those things are, big things, middle things, little things, I know we're bigger and greater than anything we meet along the way and we instinctively confront, bear down on and conquer anything that ails the collective soul.

I know I'm part of everything. I'm part of nature and I know nature doesn't worry. Imagine nature worryin', imagine the earth worryin' itself off its axis. Ha! Sometimes I'll worry a little 'bout someone if I care for 'em a lot. Like if my wife goes out and comes home hours after she said she would. Or like the time my youngest had to be rushed to the hospital.

But most worryin' is counterproductive, a waste of valuable time and just plain silly. If one morning I just happen to wake up seriously ill, I better have some seriously happy doctors working on me. I don't need worried faces reminding me I'm sick. If something in your life needs changing, worryin' won't change it, acting will. When you see something in this world that bothers you, and there's plenty in this world worth botherin' about, letting it get to you won't help you get to it.

Just do your best to be happy. Happiness doesn't require much, just an easy attitude 'bout yourself and life, a few interests, some people who love you and doing things that make you feel good. I'm just happy waking up, waking up makes me *soooo* happy. I turn over and kiss my wife, that makes me happy. I read books, that makes me happy. Home makes me happy. You get the idea? *Do* you?

Here's a little song I wrote.

You might want to sing it note for note.

DON'T WORRY

13

In every life
    we have some trouble,
But when you worry
    you make it DOUBLE.

Don't Worry,
Be Happy

Ain't got no place
to lay your head,
somebody came and
took your bed.

DON'T WORRY, BE HAPPY!

The landlord say your rent is late, he may have to litigate.

DON'T WORRY BE HAPPY!

Look at me. I'm happy.

Here, I give you my phone number.
When you worry, CALL me. I make you happy.

Ain't got no cash,
 ain't got no style,
ain't got no gal
 to make you smile.

DON'T WORRY, BE HAPPY!

'Cause when you worry
  your face will frown
and that will bring
  everybody down.

DON'T
WORRY,
BE
HAPPY!

DON'T
WORRY,
BE
HAPPY!

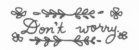

Don't worry.

Don't worry

DON'T DO iT.

BE HAPPY

Put a smile on your face

DON'T

    BRING

        EVERYBODY

            DOWN.

Don't Worry.

It will soon pass, what ever it is.

DON'T WORRY.

Be Happy

Now there is the song I wrote, I hope you learn it note for note.

In your life
expect some trouble,
when you worry
you make it double.

DON'T WORRY, BE HAPPY!

DON'T WORRY, BE HAPPY!

DON'T WORRY, BE HAPPY!

DON'T WORRY, BE HAPPY!

DON'T WORRY, BE HAPPY!

Double shifts
and overtime,
but you come home
without a dime.

Don't
Worry,
Be Happy!

Traffic gridlock
   is hard to bear,
you lost your patience,
   you lost your hair.

DON'T
WORRY
BE
HAPPY!

WRLY
RADIO

Gas, electric,
    water, too,
the bills they got
    a hold on you.

You just moved in, there's no hot water, the elevator's out of order.

DON'T WORRY, BE HAPPY!

COMPLAINTS 91ST. FL.

You just washed
the kitchen floor,
the muddy kids run
through the door.

When your heart's full of worry there can be

no room for love or serenity.

Clean floors NEVER shine like dirty happy kids.

Don't Worry Be Happy

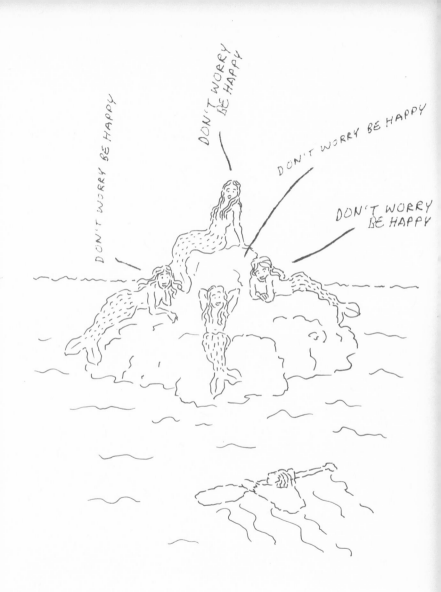

You figure that
    your raise is due,
then they go
    and fire you.

Will worrying make you rich?

In the diner
you sit and stare,
you need someone
who can care.

You met a guy,
   now you're his lover,
but he's still living
   with his mother.

DON'T WORRY, BE HAPPY!

English, physics,
math, and chem —
your son is failing
all of them.

But he's a good boy
he studies so hard!

Interviews can be a strain, but that's the price you pay for fame.

DON'T WORRY, BE HAPPY!

Umm...

The blues may come,
   that much we know,
but here's a way
   to make them go.

We're working things out.

THEY PLAY MUZAK
ON THE BEACH HERE!

You need a rest,
    get away from it all,
your secret retreat's
    now a shopping mall.

Hey!
BUY STUFF

BIG
BIZ

DON'T
WORRY,
BE
HAPPY!

These kids need new batteries.

You drag the kids
all over town,
their feet don't work,
they've got you down.

"DON'T WORRY,
-BE-
HAPPY!"

Here's a use for worry:
  it's first-rate
when you want
  to procrastinate.

Out of friends
  and all alone,
No one's there
  who you can phone.

THE WORLD'S A FRIENDLY PLACE WHEN
YOU'RE NOT WORRIED.
LOOK AROUND YOU. TELL A JOKE.
DON'T WORRY. BE HAPPY.

Your favorite show
is on TV,
but the picture's snowy,
you can hardly see

"Maybe if I put on
my 3-D glasses."

DON'T WORRY, BE HAPPY!

You thought the film
had a children's rating,
until the actors
started mating.

DON'T

BE

Drats and rats
and darns and curses,
I wrote this song,
but I'm out of verses.

You buy a second
home in Crete,
your in-laws retire
across the street.

DON'T WORRY, BE HAPPY!

Remember, life may be
short or long,
keep it happy!
Sing this song.

WORRY,

HAPPY!

I'm not worried.

I'm happy.